1914

POETRY REMEMBERS

1914

Poetry Remembers

edited by

CAROL ANN DUFFY

FABER & FABER

First published in 2013
by Faber and Faber Ltd
Bloomsbury House
74–77 Great Russell Street
London WC1B 3DA
This paperback edition first published in 2014

Typeset by RefineCatch Ltd, Bungay, Suffolk
Printed in England by CPI Group (UK) Ltd, Croydon, CR0 4YY

A CIP record for this book
is available from the British Library

ISBN 978–0–571–30215–4

2 4 6 8 10 9 7 5 3 1

CONTENTS

Introduction

'Does anybody know what it was all for?' writes Elaine Feinstein in her poem here in memory of the poet Isaac Rosenberg. A century on, the First World War – which, by the political decisions of its aftermath, spawned the Second World War only twenty-one years later – continues to cast its long, cold shadow from the past to the present. In modern-day Belgium and France, the 'iron harvest' of unexploded bombs, shrapnel, bullets and the crude, lethally effective barbed wire recalled here by Sean Borodale in his choice of an anonymous trench song, is annually uncovered by farmers during their spring planting and autumn ploughing in mind-numbing quantity. This global war, centred on Europe, mobilised over sixty-five million men. Ten million of them died and nearly twenty million were wounded; seven million civilian lives were lost: gross statistics which can only, perhaps, be comprehended, in simply human terms, through the poetry of the time.

In this memorial anthology, I have invited some of our best contemporary poets to help us remember the tragedy of the Great War by responding in new poems to the poetry, or other texts, which emerged from those four barbaric years of violence and slaughter; when Science and Politics became servants to War. Perhaps we should recall, also, the words of the philosopher and conscientious objector – a different bravery – Bertrand Russell:

And all this madness, all this rage, all this flaming death of our civilisation and our hopes, has been brought about because a set of official gentlemen, living luxurious lives, mostly stupid, and all without imagination or heart, have chosen that it should occur rather than that any one of them should suffer some infinitesimal rebuff to his country's pride.

As the voices of the living and the dead mingle in these pages, in poetry, translation or diary, it is impossible not to be brought closer to the suffering of the time. There are vivid family connections here, in new poems by Roy Fisher, Paul Muldoon, Seamus Heaney and Jackie Kay. The selections juxtapose poems by Apollinaire, Akhmatova and Hedd Wyn alongside the poems of Sassoon, Brooke, Gurney, Thomas and Owen, which are as familiar to us as hymns. And in the reference to modern conflicts by Imtiaz Dharker and Blake Morrison, however calmly uttered, we hear the proper note of outrage which all remembrance of the carnage of this War should contain, which the brave dead of all nations deserve, and which we hear clearly, still, in Siegfried Sassoon's declaration against 'the sufferings'.

I would like to thank all the poets for their commitment to ensuring that poetry remembers 1914.

CAROL ANN DUFFY

1914

POETRY REMEMBERS

CAROL ANN DUFFY

An Unseen

I watched love leave, turn, wave, want not to go,
depart, return;
late spring, a warm slow blue of air, old-new.
Love was here; not; missing, love was there;
each look, first, last.

Down the quiet road, away, away, towards
the dying time,
love went, brave soldier, the song dwindling;
walked to the edge of absence; all moments going,
gone; bells through rain

to fall on the carved names of the lost. I saw
love's child uttered,
unborn, only by rain, then and now, all future
past, an unseen. Has forever been then? Yes,
forever has been.

The Send-off

Down the close darkening lanes they sang their way
To the siding-shed,
And lined the train with faces grimly gay.

Their breasts were stuck all white with wreath and spray
As men's are, dead.

Dull porters watched them, and a casual tramp
Stood staring hard,
Sorry to miss them from the upland camp.

Then, unmoved, signals nodded, and a lamp
Winked to the guard.

So secretly, like wrongs hushed-up, they went.
They were not ours:
We never heard to which front these were sent;

Nor there if they yet mock what women meant
Who gave them flowers.

Shall they return to beating of great bells
In wild train-loads?
A few, a few, too few for drums and yells,

May creep back, silent, to village wells,
Up half-known roads.

chosen by CAROL ANN DUFFY

After the News

We sat in the garden
as if we'd been turned to stone
and the high voices of the children reached us
from the garden next door.

The bees were at their ceaseless work
in the heat of the summer's day.

I thought of a statue I saw once:
the ancient Irish saint, Fiachra,
patron of gardeners and gardens

and all they enfold, protector of bees
and the labour of their honey, their wax,
the ancient solace of candlelight in darkness.

And the story told me
that such was the saint's compassion
for the hurt and broken ones

his salt tears could heal the creatures
and restore the damaged to a wholeness again.

Before the summer comes round again,
and the birds begin to sing again

we will cry such an ocean of tears
as will break even the stone hearts of statues
where they stand on their pedestals

in the churches, in the gardens,
on the chartered streets of the city,

before the great cycle comes round again
and the bees once more
work their sweetness from the garden.

ANNA AKHMATOVA

July 1914

I

It smells of burning. For four weeks
The dry peat bog has been burning.
The birds have not even sung today,
And the aspen has stopped quaking.

The sun has become God's displeasure,
Rain has not sprinkled the fields since Easter.
A one-legged stranger came along
And all alone in the courtyard he said:

'Fearful times are drawing near. Soon
Fresh graves will be everywhere.
There will be famine, earthquakes, widespread death,
And the eclipse of the sun and the moon.

But the enemy will not divide
Our land at will, for himself:
The Mother of God will spread her white mantle
Over this enormous grief.'

8

II

The sweet smell of juniper
Flies from the burning woods.
Soldiers' wives are wailing for the boys.
The widow's lament keens over the countryside.

The public prayers were not in vain,
The earth was yearning for rain!
Warm red liquid sprinkled
The trampled fields.

Low, low hangs the empty sky
And a praying voice quietly intones:
'They are wounding your sacred body,
They are casting lots for your robes.'

July 20, 1914, Slepnyovo

translated by JUDITH HEMSCHEMEYER

chosen by PAULA MEEHAN

High Wood

15th September 1916

The bearers were quiet
carrying sections on stretchers,
forms letting out heat
grew dark in the dark.
Through the roar,
the small, piercing, chafed flutes
at the holes of throats
blew from the loss;
hands separated, tangled in wire,
feeding machinery –
the tanks were big clowns of 30-tonne iron.

Today, they still run at slow-speed,
those vaporous men through an endless
river of air,
rushing like swifts
passing the world as it arrives and leaves.
At every point of turning in
are the missing shadows,
those who have joined the shadow
from the violation, the breath
shivered into a sphere,

a bubble of torn pressures; some of its excess
enters the audio and periscopes
of hours,
scrapes the rags in the hangars of trees
and on every hill,
rattles with strewn thin off-course
homeless pieces;
strands of men.

Hanging on the Old Barbed Wire

Trench song from the First World War

If you want to find the old battalion,
I know where they are, I know where they are,
   I know where they are.
If you want to find the old battalion, I know where they are,
They're hanging on the old barbed wire.
I've seen 'em, I've seen 'em, hanging on the old barbed wire.
I've seen 'em, I've seen 'em, hanging on the old barbed wire.

chosen by SEAN BORODALE

RACHAEL BOAST

The Testament of Jean Cocteau

I have assumed the attitude of Mars when he has
an appointment with Venus
— APOLLINAIRE

From Apollinaire's star-shaped head wound
grew your signature, flower of shrapnel,
mercurial flower, the fatal hurt of a moment's fire

bursting into life – for such is art, and such
the calligram of its five petals of resistance
seeping into the edge of an age

to indicate that sometimes,
instead of closing, a wound stays open
and speaks – and so the star continues

turning itself into a flower, and the flower
into words, delicate testimonies of distances
such as those that remain when others

leave us, or take an age to arrive – star
that doesn't know the meaning of goodbye,
only the words *see you* or *night sky*

GUILLAUME APOLLINAIRE

Calligram for Madeleine (15 May 1915)

The sky's as blue and black as ink
My eyes drown in it and sink

Darkness a shell whines over me
I write this under a willow tree

translated by OLIVER BERNARD

'We bid farewell to a whole era'

Shut up Mouth you growth
You meat-eating flower
You interminable opening

Now is the hour
To find the impersonal centre of speech
And speak it freely

Lay aside your licking and pursing
And picking your thought-steps carefully across the breath
   like a cat in wet weather

Say O

As if a single ring of Hope had been sliced from the heart

The woods have taken down their flags
The flowers their hoods

Poor
Old
Rim

Of a spinning sound like a car wheel stuck in a field
That goes on turning and trying

       Surely now
       You should

          Stop
           !

GUILLAUME APOLLINAIRE

The Little Auto

On the 31st of the month of August 1914
I left Deauville not long before midnight
In Rouveyre's little auto

Counting his chauffeur there were three of us

We bid farewell to a whole era
Furious giants were rising up over Europe
Eagles were leaving their aeries waiting for the sun
Voracious fish were swimming up from the abysses
Peoples came running to get to know one another better
The dead were shaking with fear in their dark dwellings

Dogs were barking over where the borders were
I left carrying with me inside me all those armies that were
    fighting
I could feel them rising inside me and rolling out the lands
    their columns were snaking through
With the orests the happy villages of Belgium
Francorchamps with Eau Rouge the Red River and the
    pouhons springs
The region the invasions have always passed through
Railroad arteries where those who were marching off to die
Saluted life's colours one last time

17

Deep oceans where monsters were shuddering
Among the ancient shipwreck carcasses
Unimaginable heights where man fights
Higher than the eagle can soar
Man fights man up there
And falls without warning like a shooting star
Inside me I could feel some dexterous new beings
Building and also furnishing a new universe
A merchant of unbelievable opulence and prodigious size
Was setting out his fabulous wares
And gigantic shepherds were leading
Huge dumb flocks that were grazing on the speeches
And along the road all the dogs were barking at them

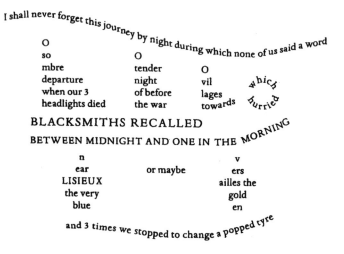

I shall never forget this journey by night during which none of us said a word

O
so   O
mbre   tender   O
departure   night   vil   which
when our 3   of before   lages   hurried
headlights died   the war   towards

BLACKSMITHS RECALLED
BETWEEN MIDNIGHT AND ONE IN THE MORNING

n   v
ear   or maybe   ers
LISIEUX   ailles the
the very   gold
blue   en

and 3 times we stopped to change a popped tyre

And when after having passed that afternoon
Through Fontainebleau
We arrived in Paris

Just as they were posting the mobilization orders
We understood my comrade and I
That the little auto had driven us into a New Era
And although we were both already grown men
We had just been born

translated by BEVERLEY BIE BRAHIC

chosen by ALICE OSWALD

The Duration

Here they are on the beach where the boy played
for fifteen summers, before he grew too old
for French cricket, shrimping and rock pools.

Here is the place where he built his dam
year after year. See, the stream still comes down
just as it did, and spreads itself on the sand

into a dozen channels. How he enlisted them:
those splendid spades, those sunbonneted girls
furiously shoring up the ramparts.

Here they are on the beach, just as they were
those fifteen summers. She has a rough towel
ready for him. The boy was always last out of the water.

She would rub him down hard, chafe him like a foal
up on its legs for an hour and trembling, all angles.
She would dry carefully between his toes.

Here they are on the beach, the two of them
sitting on the same square of mackintosh,
the same tartan rug. Quality lasts.

There are children in the water, and mothers patrolling
the sea's edge, calling them back
from the danger zone beyond the breakers.

How her heart would stab when he went too far out.
Once she flustered into the water, shouting
until he swam back. He was ashamed of her then.

Wouldn't speak, wouldn't look at her even.
Her skirt was sopped. She had to wring out the hem.
She wonders if Father remembers.

Later, when they've had their sandwiches
she might speak of it. There are hours yet.
Thousands, by her reckoning.

CYNTHIA ASQUITH

from Diaries 1915–1918

I am beginning to rub my eyes at the prospect of peace. I think it will require more courage than anything that has gone before . . . One will have to look at long vistas again, instead of short ones, and one will at last fully recognise that the dead are not only dead for the duration of the war.

chosen by HELEN DUNMORE

Gottfried Benn, *c.*1916

I'd rather speak it than write it, rather mutter it than speak it
(disobliging spiffy mutter that no one would understand)

how a man – the thing stiffened; the rogue state
familiarly engorged, bristling, crystalline; Myrmidon formation,

Schlieffen plan; Prussia the North Korea of the age,
four wars in fifty years, colonies in the Pacific everywhere not
    nailed down in 1880 –

and our man, himself to himself, the run of eleven rooms,
potters, if he cares to (not even *Uniformpflicht*), in pyjamas and
    cardigan

neither coward nor conchie, not stricken with disorder, disaffection,
    good fortune
or even medicine (medicine his sicknote), just immeasurable distance,

distance and *froideur*, an antipathy to concerted action and human
    history
beyond the dreams of Keaton or Trakl or Archimedes or Schwejk,

smokes and thinks and writes (*beguinage*, he calls it)
in his personal monastery in plucky little Belgium.

23

GOTTFRIED BENN

from Epilogue

I took my license as a doctor, researched, wrote papers on diabetes
in the army, vaccinations for gonorrhoea, peritonitis, cancer
statistics, received the Gold Medal from the University of Berlin
for some research on epilepsy; what I composed by way of literature
was written, apart from 'Morgue' which was published by A. R.
Meyer in 1912, in the spring of 1916 in Brussels. I was a doctor in a
hospital for prostitutes, a very isolated post, lived in a sequestrated
villa, shared eleven rooms with my orderly, had little to do, was
allowed to wear civvies, wasn't bothered with anything, wasn't
attached to anyone, hardly understood the language; wandered
through the streets, among strangers; a strange spring, three
incomparable months, every day I heard the bombardment on the
Yser, what did I care, life was bounded in a sphere of silence and
lostness, I lived on the edge where existence ceases and the self
begins. I often think back on those weeks; they were life, they'll not
come back, everything else was garbage.

translated and chosen by MICHAEL HOFMANN

The Crowded Earth

A million friends have flipped their backs,
words blown off and limbs vestigial.
His hands are bent against his waist
like fins in the petrified sea, as he sinks
towards a beginning neither he nor I believed in:
the instant, the flash, the bang.

I do not cry. As I open my door into snow
a woman jostles me, walks on. Words are smithereens
and beyond my skills to mend. Life is stripped
to the letter, the N . . . N . . . N of loneliness
the V . . . V . . . V of love. Friends turn to hide
their tearless faces and I do the same.

In my nurse's uniform I swim among fresh
failures of the broken earth. They flail
and moan as if born today, unwillingly.
Most soon drift to the sea-bed, their little fins curled.
A few – not him – we drag to the surface, and teach
to move among us, their eyes bright and glazed.

VERA BRITTAIN

from Testament of Youth

With November began the rainy season, when nights of thunder and fierce lightning followed copper-red sunsets, and tremendous gales left the sea with a swept and garnished appearance which filled us with dread for the ships in the Mediterranean. The furious wind blew the rain with such violence into the open verandah that water ricocheted off the stone walls and floors in a constant splash, and we were obliged to go on duty clad in black mackintoshes, gum-boots and sou'-westers.

'The doors and shutters are always blowing open and letting in a chill blast heavy with rain,' I wrote to my mother. 'One often wakes at night to hear the wind howling, the sea raging and the rain coming down with the sound of an express train rushing past. Having one's meals in the mess tent . . . is like sitting under a wet umbrella; the rain rattles on the canvas above, occasionally leaking through on to your head; tent poles and lights sway together till one feels confused and sleepy, and the water comes in at the sides of the tent and runs under the tables.'

About the middle of the month Edward's sick-leave ended, and he returned to light duty with the 3rd Sherwood Foresters at Cleadon Hutments, near Sunderland. A letter came from him, mentioning a new British attack against the German front line at Thiepval and Beaumont Hamel, just after I had been to Pietà Cemetery, the military burial-ground on the road from Valletta to Hamrun, to find the grave of one of the Buxton boys who had been buried among the purple bougainvillæa and the little stiff cypresses after dying at Cottonera Hospital from typhoid contracted in Gallipoli. To his mother in Buxton I sent a carefully wrapped pink geranium picked from his grave before I opened Edward's sad little note briefly describing the end of the two friends who had been with him on the Somme.

'Captain H.'s body was found quite close to the old front line of July 1st. E. of Authuille Wood as far as I know but I should think it was hardly recognisable. . . . N. was hit in the head by a sniper after capturing the German front line at Le Sars on Oct. 1st; he is buried in Peake Wood near Contalmaison.'

In the midst of the fear-inspiring gales, it was hard to believe that I should see my beloved three again before they had joined those friends in the crowded earth.

chosen by POLLY CLARK

Note: In 1916, Vera Brittain served with the Voluntary Aid Detachment in Malta; her 'beloved three' were her friends Victor Richardson and Geoffrey Thurlow, who died in combat at Arras in 1917, and her brother Edward Brittain, killed on the Italian Front in 1918. – PC

PAUL MULDOON

Dromedaries and Dung Beetles

An eye-level fleck of straw in the mud wall
is almost as good as gold . . .
I've ventured into this piss-poor urinal
partly to escape the wail
of thirty milch camels with their colts

as they're readied for our trek
across the dunes, partly because I've guzzled
three glasses of the diuretic
gunpowder tea the Tuareg
hold in such esteem. Their mostly business casual

attire accented by a flamboyant
blue or red nylon grab-rope
round their lower jaws, dromedaries point
to a 9 to 5 life of knees bent
in the service of fetching carboys

and carpetbags from A to B across the scarps.
Think Boyne coracles
bucking from wave to wave. Think scarab
beetles rolling their scrips
of dung to a gabfest. These dromedary-gargoyles

are at once menacing and meek
as, railing against their drivers' kicks and clicks,
they fix their beautiful-ugly mugs
on their own Meccas.
The desert sky was so clear last night the galaxies

could be seen to pulse . . .
The dromedaries were having a right old chinwag,
each musing on its bolus.
Every so often one would dispense some pills
that turned out to be generic

sheep or goat. The dung beetles set great store
not by the bitter cud
nor the often implausible *Histories*
of Herodotus but the stars
they use to guide

themselves over the same sand dunes
as these thirty milch camels
and their colts. They, too, make a continuous
line through Algeria and Tunisia.
Dung beetles have been known to positively gambol

on the outskirts of Zagora, a boom
town where water finds it hard not to gush
over the date-palms.
Despite the clouds of pumice
above Marrakesh even I might find my way to Kesh,

in the ancient Barony of Lurg,
thanks to Cassiopeia
and her self-regard. Think of how there lurks
in almost all of us a weakness for the allegorical.
Think of a Moroccan swallow's last gasp

near the wattle-and-daub oppidum
where one of my kinsmen clips
the manes of a groaning chariot-team . . .
Think of Private Henry Muldoon putting his stamp
on the mud of Gallipoli

on August 8 1915. It appears
he worked as a miner at Higham Colliery
before serving in the Lancasters and the 8th Welsh Pioneers.
His somewhat pronounced ears
confirm his place in the family gallery.

'It's only a blink,' my father used to say . . . 'Only a blink.'
I myself seem to have developed the gumption
to stride manfully out of a Neo-Napoleonic
latrine and play my part in the march on Casablanca
during the North African campaign.

The Soldier

If I should die, think only this of me:
  That there's some corner of a foreign field
That is for ever England. There shall be
  In that rich earth a richer dust concealed;
A dust whom England bore, shaped, made aware,
  Gave, once, her flowers to love, her ways to roam,
A body of England's, breathing English air,
  Washed by the rivers, blest by suns of home.

And think, this heart, all evil shed away,
  A pulse in the eternal mind, no less
    Gives somewhere back the thoughts by England given;
Her sights and sounds; dreams happy as her day;
  And laughter, learnt of friends; and gentleness,
    In hearts at peace, under an English heaven.

chosen by PAUL MULDOON

Afterbirth

Pain is lonely.
It is nothing to do with goodness.
The night you were born, I barely thought of love:
I could not think beyond pain's edges, how it moved
in a steady shudder through me, looting and burning;
how words decomposed in my mouth to brute noise.
I was naked, on all-fours. I was shitting.
There was a lull
and blood plop-plopped on the floor.
Was it mine or yours? There was a you, you
locked in struggle with me,
mortal and writhing to be out.
Then your fierce squall, the caul's net,
you clambering blind to my breast –
my tiny beautiful foe, blood-smeared.
The vast placenta slopped out, raw and ugly,
and the pain went, we slipped its trap,
we clung to each other in a truce.

'You're safe now,' I lied, I couldn't help it,
though they said you were a boy
and we know what sons are for.
They will tell you that war
is the same kind of suffering, the kind you must endure

to get to love, our wanted world, but I do not
want it without you.
You can't have been made just to be unmade,
all these slow months, these sleepless nights,
as you gnaw my spluttering breast, grow drip by drip,
your slender fingers; your sweet, wet mouth –
and death is so relentless, so grim,
what use is it to you?
It's mud that fills the throat.

It's 3 a.m. Your warm head flops to my chest.
Out there our guns bang, a boy slumps
blood-smeared, clambering blind, he cannot
think beyond war's edges, and a shudder
moves steadily to his mother
as the world squanders his body:
its painstaking work.

Afterwards

Oh, my beloved, shall you and I
Ever be young again, be young again?
The people that were resigned said to me
– Peace will come and you will lie
Under the larches up in Sheer,
Sleeping,
And eating strawberries and cream and cakes –
    O cakes, O cakes, O cakes, from Fuller's!
And quite forgetting there's a train to town,
Plotting in an afternoon the new curves for the world.

And peace came. And lying in Sheer
I look round at the corpses of the larches
Whom they slew to make pit-props
For mining the coal for the great armies.
And think, a pit prop cannot move in the wind,
Nor have red manes hanging in spring from its branches,
And sap making the warm air sweet.
Though you planted it out on the hill again it would
    be dead.

And if these years have made you into a pit-prop,
To carry the twisting galleries of the world's
    reconstruction

(Where you may thank God, I suppose
That they set you the sole stay of a nasty corner)
What use is it to you? What use
To have your body lying here
In Sheer, underneath the larches?

chosen by CLARE POLLARD

THEO DORGAN

A Munster Fusilier on his Eightieth Birthday

Coiled fire to haul back in the bolt,
weight in the stock, to cheek fitted,
to groove in the shoulder,
the long weight wedded to steel,
skeletal in my arms at night,
cold comfort, ragged and shredded sleep.
Spitfire by day, desperate and loud,
mouth with mud plugged.
Cold kiss in the spark of it,
long and percussive voice of it.

Not understanding the cold shearing,
the pare back to bone, to wood –
brittle the ash, the chestnut, the stock
and box, caissons in splinter.
And rough wool soaked in its fluids
and half-rot; dull metal the badge,
the wire in your face rust-pocked;
the blood, yes, that and the shit underfoot.
And phosphorous bright in the flesh,
what was heart, spleen, lung, bone

and belonged inside outside now,
outside everywhere raining in acres
the stuff of earth itself gleaming unearthly,
the bile in the throat waking and sleeping
the bite of it acid and stink –
stark as the thunder morning and night,
the blanketing thunder, lead plugs
at impossible speed in non-stop
drenches of rain, bee clouds of lead
furious and mindless and swarming.

And the fear, yes, bones gone to water,
the fear and, far-off, stereoscopic bright,
a hand over a body deep in mud,
in the morning air a flower in the respite,
blue to the bone, flower in a sleeve
straight up in the morning air, the body
gone down forever under in mud, shit,
blood, bone, viscera and loam –
a lone, stark hand.
It clenches once, your own.

ROBERT GRAVES

A Dead Boche

To you who'd read my songs of War
  And only hear of blood and fame,
I'll say (you've heard it said before)
  'War's Hell!' and if you doubt the same,
To-day I found in Mametz Wood
A certain cure for lust of blood:

Where, propped against a shattered trunk,
  In a great mess of things unclean,
Sat a dead Boche; he scowled and stunk
  With clothes and face a sodden green,
Big-bellied, spectacled, crop-haired,
Dribbling black blood from nose and beard.

chosen by THEO DORGAN

Stopping with a bicycle on a hill above Stroud, thinking of Ivor Gurney

Five valleys splay below me
like a broken hand encased in mud.
From this high point, I see
open veins of streams running
in rivulets toward the Severn's
metallic, distant slice of light and water.

I stand beside a hedgerow
that's been growing cancerous for years
from the broken wall my bike
is parked against. It was shrub
and bramble when I cycled past it
lazy on my way to school.

It rages, now, like a negative of fire
held still against the winter sky,
and I think of Gurney casting back
from Flanders with his pen
at a different angle, to take the same
landscape in, as if it were breath.

*

The road is quiet. No traffic
on the way from Bisley. Only buzzards
and the ghosts of babies
whose un-christened road-deaths, centuries back,
formed the town below. A new form,
the 'perfections / of flowers and petal and blade'.

But landscapes shift. Wild spaces
are surrounded. They look starker for it,
stranger, briefly, until litter intercedes.
Mankind's interactions wane and wax;
old walls collapse, new ones
clatter up the sky like angry pigeons.

*

A sheep in the field turns to bleat at me,
as if surprised by the tyrannies of change.
What would we recognise,
Gurney and I? The Severn's progress,
like a scarred, unbroken sword
shot through with filigrees of winter light.

The aching yell of gulls
flown eastward after ploughs. The way
the sun sinks like a cuticle
into a skin of cloud. The foreboding sense,
something new we can't be part of.
What rides this dusk like a pheromone.

The bicycle calls me to the hill, the wind,
the last hawk-dive into Friday night. No more
listening to spectres; no more pauses
on cold hills to mourn the sun.
'. . . the earth that ploughs
forgets protestation in its turning . . .'

IVOR GURNEY

Ballad of the Three Spectres

As I went up by Ovillers
   In mud and water cold to the knee,
There went three jeering, fleering spectres,
   That walked abreast and talked of me.

The first said, 'Here's a right brave soldier
   That walks the dark unfearingly;
Soon he'll come back on a fine stretcher,
   And laughing for a nice Blighty.'

The second, 'Read his face, old comrade,
   No kind of lucky chance I see;
One day he'll freeze in mud to the marrow,
   Then look his last on Picardie.'

Though bitter the word of these first twain
   Curses the third spat venomously;
'He'll stay untouched till the war's last dawning
   Then live one hour of agony.'

Liars the first two were. Behold me
   At sloping arms by one – two – three;
Waiting the time I shall discover
   Whether the third spake verity.

chosen by ADAM HOROVITZ

Avalon

To the Metropolitan Police Force, London:
the asylum gates are locked and chained, but undone
by wandering thoughts and the close study of maps.
So from San Francisco, patron city of tramps,
I scribble this note, having overshot Gloucester
by several million strides, having walked on water.

City of sad foghorns and clapboard ziggurats,
of snakes-and-ladders streets and cadged cigarettes,
city of pelicans, fish-bones and flaking paint,
of underfoot cable-car wires strained to breaking point . . .
I eat little – a beard of grass, a pinch of oats –
let the salt-tide scour and purge me inside and out,
but my mind still phosphoresces with lightning strikes
and I straddle each earthquake, one foot either side
of the faultline, rocking the world's seesaw.
At dusk, the Golden Gate Bridge is heaven's seashore:
I watch boats heading home with the day's catch
or ferrying souls to glittering Alcatraz,
or I face west and let the Pacific slip
in bloodshot glory over the planet's lip,
sense the waterfall at the end of the journey.

I am, ever your countryman, Ivor Gurney.

43

IVOR GURNEY

First Time In

The Captain addressed us. Afterglow grew deeper,
Like England, like the west country, and stars grew thicker.
In silence we left the billet, we found the hard roadway
In single file, jangling (silent) and on the grey
Chipped road, moaned over ever by snipers' shots.
Got shelter in the first trench; and the thud of boots
On duck-board wood from grate on rough road stone it changed.
(Verey lights showed ghastly, and a machine-gun ranged.)
Sentry here and there. How the trench wound now! Wires
Hindered, thistles pricked, but few guns spat their fires.
Upward a little . . . wider a little, the reserve line reached.
Tin hat shapes, dark body shapes and faces as bleached.
And the heart's beat: 'Here men are maimed and shot through,
    hit through;
Here iron and lead rain, sandbags rent in two;
And the honours are earned. The stuff of tales is woven.'
Here were whispers of encouragement, about the cloven
Trenches faces showed and west soft somethings were said.
Lucky were signallers who (intellectual) strangely had
Some local independence in line danger, but
In training or on Rest were from honour shut.
Bundling over sky lines to clear trench digging –
On the Plain scorn went with tapping and flag wagging
Directions. And then one took us courteously

44

Where a sheet lifted, and gold light cautiously
Streamed from an oilsheet slitted vertical into
Half-light of May. We entered, took stranger-view
Of life as lived in the line, the line of war and daily
Papers, despatches, brave-soldier talks, the really, really
Truly line, and these the heroes of story.

Never were quieter folk in teaparty history.
Never in 'Cranford', Trollope, even. And, as it were, home
Closed round us. They told us lore, how and when did come
Minnewerfers and grenades from over there east;
The pleasant and unpleasant habits of the beast
That crafted and tore Europe. What line-mending was
When guns centred and dug-outs rocked in a haze
And hearing was difficult – (wires cut) – all necessary
Common-sense workmanlike cautions of salutary
Wisdom – the mechanic day-lore of modern war-making,
Calm thought discovered in mind and body shaking.
The whole craft and business of bad occasion.
Talk turned personal, and to borders of two nations
Gone out; Cotswold's Black Mountain edges against august
August after-sun's glow, and air a lit dust
With motes and streams of gold. Wales her soul visible
Against all power west Heaven ever could flood full.
And of songs – the 'Slumber Song', and the soft Chant
So beautiful to which Rabelaisian songs were meant
Of South and North Wales; and 'David of the White Rock':
What an evening! What a first time, what a shock
So rare of home-pleasure beyond measure
And always to time's ending surely a treasure.

*

Since after-war so surely hurt, disappointed men
Who looked for the golden Age to come friendly again.
With inn evenings of meetings in warm glows,
Talk: coal and wood fire uttering rosy shows
With beer and 'Widdicombe Fair' and five mile homeward –
Moonlight lying thick on frost spangled fleet foot sward,
And owl crying out every short while his one evil word.

At any rate, disputeless the romantic evening was –
The night, the midnight; next day Fritz strafed at us,
And I lay belly upward to wonder: when – but useless.

chosen by SIMON ARMITAGE

ALAN JENKINS

The Jumps

The thin, loose-fitting one, the cotton,
With a flower-print, perhaps –
Under it the unforgotten
Hips and haunches sway . . . *You chaps!*

Look lively! (Tightening in the throat,
Can't swallow, sour burn as when
He left her last time . . .) It was curious,
What the war did to men

And horses! – Nothing 'dry, hard' anywhere
Except in iron rows; no mud either, now, but *sand*,
Sand with its 'suggestion of promenades,
Piers and bands, which entirely takes away

The sordid quality of the war'
(In the pocket of his coat
He fingers the knuckleduster Gaudier made
For him in the Frith Street years,

When he would clinch an argument
By kicking a man downstairs, and hung a furious
Wyndham Lewis by his trouser turn-ups
From the railings of Soho Square . . .)

47

*

This one, with under-arm maps of sweat;
Clings lightly to her as she wades through grass
Towards their stream. All wet.
The hot air whispers lasciviously,

The day is bright enough to blind him,
Brighter than that thing's polished brass
He used sometimes . . . On the bank below the weir
She lies and thinks of his dear 'C'

And there he is, later, with the sun behind him,
Smiling! . . .
                (Are these fighting or dancing?
Caught by a full moon's rocket flare,
In ragged twos and threes, advancing

Towards their girls all lying there
In fields of wheat or barley, hay and straw
The summer's heat has soaked into;
Who somehow, from dying there

Among coiled metal and shell-casings
Have come back to this – in full view
Of owl and fox, they kneel, and stare –
And then what shields, what interlacings!)

T. E. HULME

From Letters to Kate Lechmere

May–?September 1917

I wish I could put my hand on it. I like more than anything what you do in the morning. Do you do it every morning really. I like to think that you do . . . You know the way one hand with fingers outstretched can interlace with another with hand similarly outstretched. I like to think of our bodies like that, the x limbs being the interlacing fingers holding us close together with that whatever electric thing in the middle and with our bodies and legs as a sort of web or shield, made safe for the time being. A kind of sheltered glove for the time being inside which the delicate sucking, pumping operation can go on. . . .

I am with big guns. We get shelled almost every day, but are well protected. The man I relieved was killed by a shell, but I don't think this is at all likely to happen to me. We are very comfortable . . . I am in the sand dunes on the Belgian coast. It's a very curious life . . . all surrounded by a landscape of sand. . . .

I like being in the country. We could go one afternoon one summer, you with a cotton skirt on, *nothing* above your stockings. We'll swim like ducks and then do it. I like the hot feeling of summer . . .

chosen by ALAN JENKINS

Note: 2nd Lt. Hulme of the Royal Marine Artillery was killed by a direct hit from a shell on September 28, 1917. He was thirty-four. – AJ

49

Migration

Ledwidge was busy the day before he died,
building a lakeside road like the back-road
along the Boyne to Swynnerton from Slane.

The fowler came at break of day, and took him
from his song. The words in his head as he worked –
merle or ouzel or *lon dubh* – exploded in him.
He could not stand aside while others fought
to guard old Ireland's freedom. So he said.

There was no fence or gatepost by that road
to which he could have pinned whatever lines
might cross his mind before the short night came.

Our complement of native blackbirds
are reinforced in winter by battalions
that fly down the North Sea and Baltic
to escape the cold and then join up
with the first February chorus of the spring.

FRANCIS LEDWIDGE

Serbia

Beside the lake of Doiran
I watched the night fade, star by star,
And sudden glories of the dawn
Shine on the muddy ranks of war.

All night my dreams of that fair band
Were full of Ireland's old regret,
And when the morning filled the sky
I wondered could we save her yet.

Far up the cloudy hills, the roads
Wound wearily into the morn.
I only saw with inner eye
A poor old woman all forlorn.

chosen by BERNARD O'DONOGHUE

Boy-Soldier

The spear-point pierces his tender neck.
His armour clatters as he hits the ground.
Blood soaks his hair, bonny as the Graces',
Braids held in place by gold and silver bands.
Think of a smallholder who rears a sapling
In a beauty spot a burn burbles through
(You can hear its music close to your home)
Milky blossoms quivering in the breeze.
A spring blizzard blows in from nowhere
And uproots it, laying its branches out.
Thus Euphorbus, the son of Pantheus,
A boy-soldier – the London Scottish, say,
The Inniskillings, the Duke of Wellington's –
Was killed and despoiled by Menelaus.

TOM McALINDON

We had a young volunteer here called Bobbie Kernaghan. He said he was seventeen but looked about fifteen to me. He was just out and so keen to get at the Germans, they had killed his favourite uncle. He was from Balfour Street in Belfast and said it's a small world, a neighbour of his was an Annie O'Hagan from the Mointies. Do you know her? I straightened his pack and checked his rifle (everything we have and wear is plastered with mud) before we went up and over on the 9th. We had hardly gone ten yards when he got it in the chest. He looked like a schoolboy asleep when they brought him in and laid him down. He lay covered over in the bottom of the trench for a few days. Every time I passed him I thought of when I was seventeen and of the nine years I've had since then. You get very callous here after a while, you simply have to, but this lads death got through all my callousness. The Divisional Commander inspected us this morning and congratulated us on our 'great work at Ovillers'. Great!

chosen by MICHAEL LONGLEY

Note: Tom McAlindon served in the Royal Irish Rifles. – ML

DAVID HARSENT

Armistice

In the Peaceable Kingdom things go from bad to good
by way of a pleasant word where creatures are hand-fed

the lynx and the lamb and walk untroubled in a sunlit wood
of wild fruits and hymnal birdsong where children are led

daily to the sea of harmony and go as one head-
first to sound in boundless green where everyone is blood-

brother to someone where light is shed
hard to dispel the dark where ranks of the would-be sad

are gentled and set aside then to be cured
where blonde girls do their duty as they should

where language is trimmed to be better understood
where those who mistake the road out for the road

to recovery are helped back by a rolling barricade
of white roses and bramble where fire and flood

creep to meet and bond along the seam where food
is brought as song is brought as sleep is brought as bride

to bridegroom mother to long lost son set side by side
to music and applause where love is stalled

by pity where the crucified man steps down the sopping bud
of his heart in his outstretched hand while the dead

silence that draws out over battlefield and potter's field
is what remains of the truth of it and must be left unsaid.

JOHN McCAULEY

Such courage and nerve as I possessed were stolen from me on the blood-drenched plains of northern France . . . Devil's Trench, and many other trenches in France and Flanders, have helped to make me a weakling. They took away many of the attributes which contributed to my manhood, sapped up my courage, shattered my nerves and drew me back into a 'civilised' world again broken in spirit and in nerve, and the coward that I am. They might as well have taken my body, too.

Patriotism was rarely known and never understood in the front line . . . 'They died that England might live.' Every day I hear these words ringing in my ears, like the daily dinning of the shellfire of years ago. What if they who died could come back and survey this sorry world, and see what it was they fought for? I wonder what their thoughts would be. Perhaps they would say, 'We are better and happier in our world.'

chosen by DAVID HARSENT

Note: John McCauley was a Private in the 2nd Border Regiment. – DH

BLAKE MORRISON

Redacted

The raw material for the inquest was a substantial document . . . It was initially so
heavily redacted by the MOD that it was almost impossible to understand.
— MARGARET EVISON, Death of a Soldier

This poem has been redacted
In the interests of national security.
It's an inquest into the death of a serving officer
Heard at a Coroner's Court for the MOD.

On May 9th 20█ Lieutenant ███ ████, who had begun
His first posting, at Fort ████, just 12 days earlier,
Undertook a routine patrol with members of his platoon,
Including two guardsmen and an interpreter.

It was the aftermath of the poppy harvest
And their instructions were to dominate the █ area of Helmand,
By repelling Taliban insurgents
And winning local hearts and minds.

Five minutes after leaving base they came under fire
And took cover in a compound, behind a high mud wall,
Where Lieutenant ████ tried to radio for reinforcements,
Briefly standing in the entrance doorway to get a signal –

Which was when the bullet hit, finding the gap
Between his body armour and his collar bone
And knocking him flat on the sandy ground.
'Man down', his colleagues shouted, 'Man down'.

Guardsman ████████████ radioed for a helicopter
While Guardsman ██████, the team medic, wiped the blood
From the hole in his right shoulder (the size of a 50p coin),
Staunching the flow with a field dressing as best he could.

Still under fire, Lieutenant ███████ was placed on a stretcher
And carried through irrigation ditches back to base; the ride
Was bumpy but he kept talking as he lay there
And even asked for (and was given) a cigarette.

While awaiting the arrival of the helicopter team,
He was injected with morphine in his right thigh.
And a Hemcon bandage applied to the wound,
But his pulse was slowing – the bullet had ruptured an artery.

The Blackhawk helicopter arrived forty minutes later.
During the flight Lieutenant ███████ suffered a cardiac arrest.
And though operated on in hospital at Camp ████████
He failed to recover consciousness.

Further tests at ██████ hospital in the UK, following his transfer
By plane, confirmed the absence of brain activity.
Parents and friends spent time at his beside
Before the life support machine was turned off next day.

The poem's sympathies are with his family for their loss
But it is satisfied that everything possible was done
To save the life of Lieutenant ███████
And it therefore refutes any suggestion

That his body armour offered scant protection,
That his Bowman Radio did not work properly,
That the medical equipment supplied to the troops was inadequate,
And that the 65-minute delay

Between the bullet hitting and the helicopter landing –
The product of a communication failure or of
A navigation error on the part of the pilot –
Was what cost Lieutenant ███████ his life.

Nor can the poem judge whether his deployment
As platoon commander on his first tour of duty
In an area notorious for insurgents and snipers
Was negligent to the point of criminality.

As to claims that the war in Afghanistan is unwinnable,
That teenagers are being used as cannon fodder and that
Their deaths serve no purpose whatsoever –
To comment would be inappropriate.

In short, after hearing all the evidence,
The poem concludes that Lieutenant ███████ suffered injuries
That were regrettable but unsurvivable.
While on active service for his country,

His death being the result of 1a) necrosis of the brain
Due to 1b) major blood loss due to 1c)
A gunshot wound. Signed, ███████ █████████████, Coroner,
Acting independently for the MOD.

Recruiting

'Lads, you're wanted, go and help,'
On the railway carriage wall
Stuck the poster, and I thought
Of the hands that penned the call.

Fat civilians wishing they
'Could go and fight the Hun'.
Can't you see them thanking God
That they're over forty-one?

Girls with feathers, vulgar songs –
Washy verse on England's need –
God – and don't we damned well know
How the message ought to read.

'Lads, you're wanted! over there,'
Shiver in the morning dew,
More poor devils like yourselves
Waiting to be killed by you.

Go and help to swell the names
In the casualty lists.
Help to make the column's stuff
For the blasted journalists.

Help to keep them nice and safe
From the wicked German foe.
Don't let him come over here!
'Lads, you're wanted – out you go.'

There's a better word than that,
Lads, and can't you hear it come
From a million men that call
You to share their martyrdom?

Leave the harlots still to sing
Comic songs about the Hun,
Leave the fat old men to say
Now *we've* got them on the run.

Better twenty honest years
Than their dull three score and ten.
Lads, you're wanted. Come and learn
To live and die with honest men.

You shall learn what men can do
If you will but pay the price,
Learn the gaiety and strength
In the gallant sacrifice.

Take your risk of life and death
Underneath the open sky.
Live clean or go out quick –
Lads, you're wanted. Come and die.

chosen by BLAKE MORRISON

JOHN AGARD

Bandages

We're the timeless witnesses
to how alike all people bleed –

the swaddling white that comes
to the call of the limb in need.

We speak the language of the hurt
we weep the red of every creed

we've seen it all down the centuries
from Achilles to Baghdad –

how humankind replenishes
its tribal Iliad.

Still we blossom out of anguish
we who marry hope to wounds.

ALBERT 'SMILER' MARSHALL

I was wounded at Mametz Wood and I landed up in Rouen Hospital, with a bullet through my hand amongst other wounds. The boat bringing the wounded back docked at Newcastle, and I was sent to convalesce in Eastbourne. They dressed me in blue with a white shirt and red tie so that everyone could see that I'd been wounded.

chosen by JOHN AGARD

Note: Albert 'Smiler' Marshall was a Private in the 1st Battalion, Essex Yeomanry. — JA

March 2013

In Afghanistan, *Nauroz*, New Year, my driver says,
is Spring; an avalanche of water from the mountains.
We have snow leopards, wild goats, gray wolves,
black bears, mynah birds, rock doves, tulips,
brown veined butterflies. Three decades of war
but our foothills still flower. Summer is too hot –
I take my daughters twice a year, in Spring
and Autumn. I want them to know
where their hearts are. I try to apologise.
No, No, he says, many things are better,
my mother no longer walks for twenty miles
to reach a phone that might be broken,
my sisters can leave the house, can go to college;
but when you go, we know They will come back.
I want my girls to have an education.
Look! He stops the car. In this safe flat land,
Spring is here! He winds down his window –
the Cambridge Backs, massed with purple crocus.

CHARLOTTE MEW

May, 1915

Let us remember Spring will come again
               To the scorched, blackened woods, where the
               wounded trees
Wait with their old wise patience for the heavenly rain,
Sure of the sky: sure of the sea to send its healing breeze,
          Sure of the sun. And even as to these
               Surely the Spring, when God shall please,
          Will come again like a divine surprise
To those who sit today with their great Dead, hands in their
     hands, eyes in their eyes,
At one with Love, at one with Grief: blind to the scattered
     things and changing skies.

chosen by ANN GRAY

DALJIT NAGRA

The Calling

The night is abrim with the in-between children
they are summoning Mother India

take us back   take us back   take us back

but the Motherland is piping the old grief
I was down on my knees   on my knees

why did you run toward the moon
for the cities with their engines of desire

The night is abrim with the in-between children
their heads are down and are crying

take us back   take us back   take us back

our songs are afresh with the plough and the oxen,
the smell of open fires where the roti is crackling

and our roses are the roses of home.

The Gift of India

Is there ought you need that my hands withhold,
Rich gifts of raiment or grain or gold?
Lo! I have flung to the East and the West
Priceless treasures torn from my breast,
And yielded the sons of my stricken womb
To the drum-beats of the duty, the sabers of doom.
Gathered like pearls in their alien graves
Silent they sleep by the Persian waves,
Scattered like shells on Egyptian sands,
They lie with pale brows and brave, broken hands,
they are strewn like blossoms mown down by chance
On the blood-brown meadows of Flanders and France
Can ye measure the grief of the tears I weep
Or compass the woe of the watch I keep?
Or the pride that thrills thro' my heart's despair
And the hope that comforts the anguish of prayer?
And the far sad glorious vision I see
Of the torn red banners of victory?
when the terror and the tumult of hate shall cease
And life be refashioned on anvils of peace,
And your love shall offer memorial thanks
To the comrades who fought on the dauntless ranks,
And you honour the deeds of the dauntless ones,
Remember the blood of my martyred sons!

chosen by DALJIT NAGRA

Futility

John Donne tells the sun where to go,
Blake's flower is busy counting its steps,

and nothing like it
are the eyes of Shakespeare's girl,

but this one over France
is as real as the soldier's body lying there –

not a metaphor this time,
unless the sun is the court of last appeal.

And what we call the speaker
is really young Owen saying

his hinged poem, which quickly slips
from hope to a knot of a question

then swings us back to the title
that we knew from the start,

a thorn we carried through the poem,
but takes us still by sad surprise.

If only he knew that in world wars
we are only up to number II

and have a long way to go
before we show our final colors on a torn flag.

WILFRED OWEN

Futility

Move him into the sun –
Gently its touch awoke him once,
At home, whispering of fields half-sown.
Always it woke him, even in France,
Until this morning and this snow.
If anything might rouse him now
The kind old sun will know.

Think how it wakes the seeds –
Woke once the clays of a cold star.
Are limbs, so dear achieved, are sides
Full-nerved, still warm, too hard to stir?
Was it for this the clay grew tall?
– O what made fatuous sunbeams toil
To break earth's sleep at all?

chosen by BILLY COLLINS

A century later

The school-bell is a call to battle,
every step to class, a step
into the firing-line.
Here is the target, fine skin
at the temple, cheek still rounded
from being fifteen.

Surrendered, surrounded,
she takes the bullet in the head

and walks on. The missile cuts
a pathway in her mind,
to an orchard in full bloom,
a field humming under the sun,
its lap open and full of poppies.

This girl has won
the right to be ordinary,

wear bangles to a wedding,
paint her fingernails,
go to school.

Bullet, she says, *you are stupid.*
You have failed.

You cannot kill a book
or the buzzing in it.

A murmur, a swarm. Behind her,
one by one, the schoolgirls are standing up
to take their places on the front line.

WILFRED OWEN

Anthem for Doomed Youth

What passing-bells for these who die as cattle?
   – Only the monstrous anger of the guns.
   Only the stuttering rifles' rapid rattle
Can patter out their hasty orisons.
No mockeries now for them; no prayers nor bells;
   Nor any voice of mourning save the choirs, –
The shrill, demented choirs of wailing shells;
   And bugles calling for them from sad shires.

What candles may be held to speed them all?
   Not in the hands of boys but in their eyes
Shall shine the holy glimmers of goodbyes.
   The pallor of girls' brows shall be their pall;
Their flowers the tenderness of patient minds,
And each slow dusk a drawing-down of blinds.

chosen by IMTIAZ DHARKER

April Fools' Day

i.m. Isaac Rosenberg

Does anybody know what it was all for?
Not Private Rosenberg, short as John Keats.
A nudge from Ezra Pound took him to War,
to sleep on boards, in France, with rotting feet,
writing his poetry by candle ends.
He knew his fellow soldiers found him odd.
Outsiders never easily make friends
if they are awkward with a foreign God.

He should have stayed in Cape Town with his sister.
Did he miss Marsh's breakfasts at Grays Inn,
or Café Royal? He longed for the centre
but he was always shy round Oxbridge toffs –
He lacked the sexy eyes of Mark Gertler –
and his *Litvak* underlip could put them off.
'From Stepney East!' as Pound wrote Harriet
'Ma che!' while sending poems to her.

You died on April Fools' Day on patrol.
beyond the corpses lying in the mud,
carrying up the line a barbed wire roll
– useless against gun fire – with the blood
and flesh of Death in the Spring air.
Yours was *a life half lived*, if even that,
and the remains of it were never found. But we remember
your *iron honey gold*. Your *cosmopolitan rat*.

ISAAC ROSENBERG

Break of Day in the Trenches

The darkness crumbles away –
It is the same old druid Time as ever.
Only a live thing leaps my hand –
A queer sardonic rat –
As I pull the parapet's poppy
To stick behind my ear.
Droll rat, they would shoot you if they knew
Your cosmopolitan sympathies.
Now you have touched this English hand
You will do the same to a German –
Soon, no doubt, if it be your pleasure
To cross the sleeping green between.
It seems you inwardly grin as you pass
Strong eyes, fine limbs, haughty athletes
Less chanced than you for life,
Bonds to the whims of murder,
Sprawled in the bowels of the earth,
The torn fields of France.
What do you see in our eyes
At the shrieking iron and flame
Hurled through still heavens?
What quaver – what heart aghast?
Poppies whose roots are in man's veins
Drop, and are ever dropping;

But mine in my ear is safe,
Just a little white with the dust.

chosen by ELAINE FEINSTEIN

RUTH PADEL

Birds of the Western Front

Your mess-tin cover's lost. Kestrels hover
above the shelling. They don't turn a feather
when hunting-ground explodes in yellow earth,

flickering star-shells
and flares from the Revelation of St John.
You look away

from artillery lobbing roar and suck and snap
against one corner of a thicket
to the partridge of the war zone

making its nest in shattered clods. History
floods into subsoil to be blown apart. You cling
to the hard dry stars of observation.

How you survive. They all were at it:
Orchids of the Crimea,
nature notes from the trench

leaving everything unsaid – hell's cauldron
with souls pushed in, demons stoking flames beneath –
for the pink-flecked wings of a chaffinch

flashed like mediaeval glass.
You replace gangrene and gas mask
with a dream of alchemy: language of the birds

translating human earth
to abstract and divine. While machine-gun
tracery gutted that stricken wood

you watched the chaffinch flutter to and fro
through splintered branches, breaking buds
and never a green bough left.

Hundreds lay in there wounded.
If any, you say, spotted one small bird
they may have wondered why a thing with wings

would stay in such a place.
She must have, sure, had chicks
she was too terrified to feed, too loyal to desert.

Like roots clutching at air
you stick to the lark singing fit to bust at dawn
sounding insincere

above the burning bush: plough-land
latticed like folds of brain
with shell-ravines where nothing stirs

but black rats, jittery sentries and the lice
sliding across your faces every night.
Where every elixir's gone wrong

you hold to what you know.
A little nature study. A solitary magpie
blue and white

spearing a strand of willow.
One for sorrow. One for Babylon,
Ninevah and Northern France,

for mice and desolation, the burgeoning
barn-owl population
and never a green bough left.

SAKI

from Birds on the Western Front

Considering the enormous economic dislocation which the war operations have caused in the regions where the campaign is raging, there seems to be very little corresponding disturbance in the bird life of the same districts. Rats and mice have mobilized and swarmed into the fighting line, and there has been a partial mobilization of owls, particularly barn owls, following in the wake of the mice, and making laudable efforts to thin out their numbers. What success attends their hunting one cannot estimate; there are always sufficient mice left over to populate one's dug-out and make a parade-ground and race-course of one's face at night. In the matter of nesting accommodation the barn owls are well provided for; most of the still intact barns in the war zone are requisitioned for billeting purposes, but there is a wealth of ruined houses, whole streets and clusters of them, such as can hardly have been available at any previous moment of the world's history since Nineveh and Babylon became humanly desolate. Without human occupation and cultivation there can have been no corn, no refuse, and consequently very few mice, and the owls of Nineveh cannot have enjoyed very good hunting; here in Northern France the owls have desolation and mice at their disposal in unlimited quantities, and as these birds breed in winter as well as in summer, there should be a goodly output of war owlets to cope with the swarming generations of war mice. . . .

Kestrels hover about all day in the hottest parts of the line, not in the least disconcerted, apparently, when a promising mouse-area suddenly rises in the air in a cascade of black or yellow earth . . . The skylark has stuck tenaciously to the meadows and croplands that have been seamed and bisected with trenches and honeycombed with shell-holes. In the chill, misty hour of gloom that precedes a rainy dawn, when nothing seemed alive except a few wary water-logged sentries and many scuttling rats, the lark would suddenly dash skyward and pour forth a song of ecstatic jubilation that sounded horribly forced and insincere. It seemed scarcely possible that the bird could carry its insouciance to the length of attempting to rear a brood in that desolate wreckage of shattered clods and gaping shell-holes, but once, having occasion to throw myself down with some abruptness on my face, I found myself nearly on the top of a brood of young larks. Two of them had already been hit by something, and were in rather a battered condition, but the survivors seemed as tranquil and comfortable as the average nestling.

At the corner of a stricken wood (which has had a name made for it in history, but shall be nameless here), at a moment when lyddite and shrapnel and machine-gun fire swept and raked and bespattered that devoted spot as though the artillery of an entire Division had suddenly concentrated on it, a wee hen-chaffinch flitted wistfully to and fro, amid splintered and falling branches that had never a green bough left on them. The wounded lying there, if any of them noticed the small bird, may well have wondered why anything having wings and no pressing reason for remaining should have chosen to stay in such a place. There was a battered orchard alongside the stricken wood, and the probable explanation of the bird's presence was that it had a nest of young ones whom it was too scared to feed, too loyal to desert. Later on, a small flock of chaffinches blundered into the wood, which they were doubtless in the habit of using as a highway to their feeding-grounds; unlike the solitary hen-bird, they made no secret of their desire to get away as fast as their dazed wits would let them. The only other bird I ever saw there was a magpie, flying low over the wreckage of fallen tree-limbs; 'one for sorrow', says the old superstition. There was sorrow enough in that wood.

The English gamekeeper, whose knowledge of wild life usually runs on limited and perverted lines, has evolved a sort of religion as to the nervous debility of even the hardiest game birds; according to his beliefs a terrier trotting across a field in which a partridge is nesting, or a mouse-hawking kestrel hovering over the hedge, is sufficient cause to drive the distracted bird off its eggs and send it whirring into the next county.

The partridge of the war zone shows no signs of such sensitive nerves. The rattle and rumble of transport, the constant coming and going of bodies of troops, the incessant rattle of musketry and deafening explosions of artillery, the night-long flare and flicker of star-shells, have not sufficed to scare the local birds away from their chosen feeding grounds, and to all appearances they have not been deterred from raising their broods. Gamekeepers who are serving with the colours might seize the opportunity to indulge in a little useful nature study.

chosen by RUTH PADEL

Note: Saki was the pen name of Hector Hugh Munro, born 1870, master short-story-writer. In 1914, over-age, he refused a commission and joined up as a trooper. In November 1916 he was killed by a sniper. His last words were, 'Put that bloody cigarette out!' The essay from which these extracts come was published posthumously in 1924. – RP

Bantam

My father at 87 remembers his father at 17

It wisnae men they sent tae war.
It wis boys like the Bantams
– wee men named efter
a small breed o' chickens,
or later: a jeep, a bike, a camera.
That needy fir soldiers they drapped height
Restriction; so small men came to war.
As a prisoner, my faither's weight fell.
And years later, the shrapnel fray the Somme
Shot oot, a wee jewel hidden in his left airm.

SIEGFRIED SASSOON

Survivors

No doubt they'll soon get well; the shock and strain
   Have caused their stammering, disconnected talk.
Of course they're 'longing to go out again,' –
   These boys with old, scared faces, learning to walk.
They'll soon forget their haunted nights; their cowed
   Subjection to the ghosts of friends who died, –
Their dreams that drip with murder; and they'll be proud
   Of glorious war that shatter'd all their pride . . .
Men who went out to battle, grim and glad;
Children, with eyes that hate you, broken and mad.

Craiglockhart, October 1917

chosen by JACKIE KAY

A Moment of Reflection

28 June 1914

(*with acknowledgements to* Black Lamb and Grey Falcon
by Rebecca West)

Although one assassin has already tried
and failed to blow him to pieces,
Archduke Ferdinand has let it be known
he will soon complete his journey
as planned along the quay at Sarajevo,

but for a moment will pause
here,
at the window of a private room in the Town Hall.

He needs time to recover his composure
after finding the blood of his aide-de-camp
splattered over the manuscript of the speech
he delivered so well earlier this morning;
he needs to look around him.
And indeed,
the prospect of an Austrian brewery in the distance
is reassuring,
likewise the handsome red bricks of the barracks
filled with several thousand soldiers of the fatherland.

This is how those who survive him today
will remember him:

a man thinking his thoughts
while waiting until his wife can join him –
the Countess Chotek
with her pinched yet puddingy features,
to whom he will shortly utter his last words,
'Sophie, live for our children',
into deaf ears.

As for his own memories,
the Head of the Tourist Bureau
has now arrived and taken it upon himself
to suggest the Archduke might be happy to recall the fact
that only last week
he bagged his three thousandth stag,

Was this, the Head dares to enquire,
with the double-barrelled Mannlicher
made for him especially –
the same weapon he used to dispatch
two thousand one hundred and fifty game birds
in a single day,
and sixty boars at a hunt led by the Kaiser?

These are remarkable achievements,
the Head dares to continue,
on the same level as the improvement
the Archduke has suggested in the hunting of hare,

by which the beaters,
forming themselves into a wedge-shape,
squeeze those notoriously elusive runners
towards a particular spot
where he can exceed the tally of every other gun.

In the silence that follows
it is not obvious whether the Archduke
has heard the question.
He has heard it.
He is more interested, however,
in the fact that his mind is now stuffed
with an almost infinite number of ghosts
of woodcock, quail, pleasant and partridge,
wild boars bristling flank to flank,
mallard and teal and wild geese
dangling from the antlers of stags,
layer after layer of rabbits
and other creatures that were mere vermin –

a tally that he expects will increase
once the business of today has been accomplished.

SIEGFRIED SASSOON

I am making this statement as an act of wilful defiance of military authority, because I believe that the war is being deliberately prolonged by those who have the power to end it.

I am a soldier, convinced that I am acting on behalf of soldiers. I believe that this war, upon which I entered as a war of defence and liberation, has now become a war of aggression and conquest. I believe that the purposes for which I and my fellow-soldiers entered upon this war should have been so clearly stated as to have made it impossible to change them, and that, had this been done, the objects which actuated us would now be attainable by negotiation.

I have seen and endured the sufferings of the troops, and I can no longer be a party to prolong these sufferings for ends which I believe to be evil and unjust.

I am not protesting against the conduct of the war, but against the political errors and insincerities for which the fighting men are being sacrificed.

On behalf of those who are suffering now I make this protest against the deception which is being practised on them; also I believe that I may help to destroy the callous complacence with which the majority of those at home regard the continuance of agonies which they do not share, and which they have not sufficient imagination to realize.

chosen by ANDREW MOTION

Note: statement made to his commanding officer by 2nd Lt. S. L. Sassoon, Military Cross, 3rd Battalion Royal Welch Fusiliers, explaining his grounds for refusing to serve further in the army (Bradford Pioneer, 27 July 1917) – AM

VICKI FEAVER

Oranges

As Orcades left Greenock
dockers unloading another ship
pelted the deck with oranges.

Still subdued from goodbyes
to wives and sweethearts
and friends and families

they didn't know when, or if
they'd see again – the men
perked up: scrabbling to grab

an orange before it rolled
out of reach, or leaping to field one
before it burst on the deck.

And all the time, a band playing
and oranges raining down
like golden grenades.

GERTRUDE STEIN

Orange In

Go lack go lack use to her.
Cocoa and clear soup and oranges and oat-meal.
Whist bottom whist close, whist clothes, woodling.
Cocoa and clear soup and oranges and oat-meal.
Pain soup, suppose it is question, suppose it is butter, real is,
real is only, only excreate, only excreate a no since.
A no, a no since, a no since when, a no since when since, a no
since when since a no since when since, a no since, a no since
when since, a no since, a no, a no since a no since, a no since, a no
since.

chosen by VICKI FEAVER

JULIA COPUS

Any Ordinary Morning

i.m. Adolf Büker (d. 19th June 1918)

The world is as it is. This morning, for instance,
the primroses are out on the lawn, in clusters
of yellow and carmine; the lilac sways; the washing
ripples on the line. And when I lift
my orange juice to sip and set it down,
the same small chips of sunlight coalesce
on the side of my glass; the old shapes settle again

in the frame of the Kriegs-Chronik, your face at its centre
in black and white, boyish but serious –
too young beneath the spike of your Pickelhaube.
Around you the terrible names persist – Arras,
Verdun – the places you served in, rivers and towns
set in the thick black script of invocations:
Cambrai, Louvement, Monchy-le-Preux, the Scarpe . . .

Adolf Büker, it was not the soldier
in you but the lover who shaped my life.
I think of him now, the morning you left for war.
Your new young wife beside you doesn't know yet
how the story goes. Your final battle
tucked in the future still, she is laying the breakfast
unaware that already my sweetheart's grandmother
is safely landed inside her – meaning I live

not in some other world but here in this one
in which your great grandson returns each evening
at the end of both our working days, and the light
bounces off my glass any ordinary morning,
as I picture it now, catching the gold hairs
on your Marie's brown arms and flashing out
from her silver Kaffeekanne while she pours
another coffee into the kitchen's quiet.

SEAMUS HEANEY

In a field

And there I was in the middle of a field,
The furrows once called 'scores' still with their gloss,
The tractor with its hoisted plough just gone

Snarling at an unexpected speed
Out on the road. Last of the jobs,
The windings had been ploughed, furrows turned

Three ply or four round each of the four sides
Of the breathing land, to mark it off
And out. Within that boundary now

Step the fleshy earth and follow
The long healed footprints of one who arrived
From nowhere, unfamiliar and de-mobbed,

In buttoned khaki and buffed army boots,
Bruising the turned-up acres of our back field
To stumble from the windings' magic ring

And take me by a hand to lead me back
Through the same old gate into the yard
Where everyone has suddenly appeared,

All standing waiting.

EDWARD THOMAS

As the team's head-brass

As the team's head-brass flashed out on the turn
The lovers disappeared into the wood.
I sat among the boughs of the fallen elm
That strewed an angle of the fallow, and
Watched the plough narrowing a yellow square
Of charlock. Every time the horses turned
Instead of treading me down, the ploughman leaned
Upon the handles to say or ask a word,
About the weather, next about the war.
Scraping the share he faced towards the wood,
And screwed along the furrow till the brass flashed
Once more.
                    The blizzard felled the elm whose crest
I sat in, by a woodpecker's round hole,
The ploughman said. 'When will they take it away?'
'When the war's over.' So the talk began –
One minute and an interval of ten,
A minute more and the same interval.
'Have you been out?' 'No.' 'And don't want to, perhaps?'
'If I could only come back again, I should.
I could spare an arm. I shouldn't want to lose
A leg. If I should lose my head, why, so,
I should want nothing more. . . . Have many gone
From here?' 'Yes.' 'Many lost?' 'Yes: a good few.

Only two teams work on the farm this year.
One of my mates is dead. The second day
In France they killed him. It was back in March,
The very night of the blizzard, too. Now if
He had stayed here we should have moved the tree.'
'And I should not have sat here. Everything
Would have been different. For it would have been
Another world.' 'Ay, and a better, though
If we could see all all might seem good.' Then
The lovers came out of the wood again:
The horses started and for the last time
I watched the clods crumble and topple over
After the ploughshare and the stumbling team.

chosen by JULIA COPUS *and* SEAMUS HEANEY

For a Fatherless Son, for a Fatherless Daughter

I

Somewhere your childhood finds itself:
the music of a football kicked against a wall,
a nintendo on a park bench,
suddenly abandoned in the sun.
Now, as day slips, the meadows
where you've played all afternoon are
emptying of light. I watch
as you stretch up,
feeling for the words there are,
the lengths we find in grass and shadow
to measure growth against.

II

She feels the fullness of her body through her father's songs.
When he sings to her he sings the night's explosions,
    distant stars.
I did not think it would feel like this.
I lie all night awake and count the years.

97

HELEN THOMAS

from World Without End

So we lay, all night, sometimes talking of our love and all that had
been, and of the children, and what had been amiss and what right.
We knew the best was that there had never been untruth between
us. We knew all of each other, and it was right. So talking and
crying and loving in each other's arms we fell asleep as the cold
reflected light of the snow crept through the frost-covered widows.

Edward got up and made the fire and brought me some tea, and
then got back into bed, and the children clambered in, too, and sat
in a row sipping our tea. I was not afraid of crying any more. My
tears had been shed, my heart was empty, stricken with something
that tears would not express or comfort. The gulf had been bridged.
Each bore the other's suffering. We concealed nothing, for all was
known between us. After breakfast, while he showed me where his
account books were and what each was for, I listened calmly, and
unbelievingly he kissed me when I said I, too, would keep accounts.
'And here are my poems. I've copied them all out in this book for
you, and the last of all is for you. I wrote it last night, but don't read
it now. . . . It's still freezing. The ground is like iron, and more snow
has fallen. The children will come to the station with me; and now
I must be off.' . . .

A thick mist hung everywhere, and there was no sound except,
far away in the valley, a train shunting. I stood at the gate watching
him go; he turned back to wave until the mist and the hill hid him.
I heard his old call coming up to me: 'Coo-ee!' he called. 'Coo-ee!'

I answered, keeping my voice strong to call again. Again through the muffled air came his 'Coo-ee'. And again went my answer like an echo. 'Coo-ee' came fainter next time with the hill between us, but my 'Coo-ee' went out of my lungs strong to pierce to him as he strode away from me. 'Coo-ee!' So faint now, it might only be my own call flung back from the thick air and muffling snow. I put my hands up to my mouth to make a trumpet, but no sound came. Panic seized me, and I ran through the mist and the snow to the top of the hill, and stood there a moment dumbly, with straining eyes and ears. There was nothing but the mist and the snow and the silence of death.

Then with leaden feet which stumbled in a sudden darkness that overwhelmed me I groped my way back to the empty house.

chosen by DERYN REES-JONES

ROY FISHER

Signs and Signals

When the trench wall came away without warning
and exposed the singularly tall
German officer, set upright in the earth
as if in a raised niche and seeming
unharmed though dead, the sight –
gloves, boots, pale grey-blue greatcoat, attitude –
did its work. For Lance-Corporal (signals) Fisher W., Royal
Fusiliers, it would be the most splendid figure of a man
he'd ever see.

Battered, the cathedral at Reims went some way
towards making up for the soldiery of France
neither stoical nor sanitary.

Then on sunny days
the pleasure of making the sharp flashes of his heliograph
go skittering over the filth for miles.

GEORG TRAKL

Grodek

At nightfall the autumn woods cry out
With deadly weapons, and the golden plains
The deep blue lakes, above which more darkly
Rolls the sun; the night embraces
Dying warriors, the wild lament
Of their broken mouths.
But quietly there in the pastureland
Red clouds in which an angry god resides,
The shed blood gathers, lunar coolness.
All the roads lead to blackest carrion.
Under golden twigs of the night and stars
The sister's shade now sways through the silent copse
To greet the ghosts of the heroes, the bleeding heads;
And softly the dark flutes of autumn sound in the reeds.
O prouder grief! You brazen altars,
Today a great pain feeds the hot flame of the spirit,
The grandsons yet unborn.

translated by MICHAEL HAMBURGER

chosen by ROY FISHER

GRACE NICHOLS

At Stockwell Tube

Death followed you to the underground.
Followed you, Jean Charles de Menezes,
even onto this train – but no trace
of your blood now. No flowering stain.

Just this palpable vision
of your breath's rasping rhythm –
your small days' flashing rivers – the oblivious gun

And my own Cassandra moment:
What if it's the wrong man?
What if he's innocent?

Death followed you to the underground
to a world gone all wrong –
A metal sky
        A fabricated earth
                No carnival –

Just unstoppable Death in the shape of the law
and a mother journeying to the root of her tears.

GIUSEPPE UNGARETTI

Clear Sky

July 1918

After so much
mist
one by one
the stars
unveil

I breathe in
the cool air
that the colour of the sky
gives me

I know I am
a passing
image

Caught in an immortal
circle

translated by PATRICK CREAGH

chosen by GRACE NICHOLS

103

GILLIAN CLARKE

Eisteddfod of the Black Chair

for Hedd Wyn, 1887–1917

Robert Graves met him once,
in the hills above Harlech,
the shepherd poet,
the *awdl* and the *englyn* in his blood
like the heft of the mountain
in the breeding of his flock.

In a letter from France, he writes
of poplars whispering, the sun going down
among the foliage like an angel of fire.
and flowers half hidden in leaves
growing in a spent shell.
'Beauty is stronger than war.'

Yet he heard sorrow in the wind, foretold
blood in the rain reddening the fields
under the shadow of crows,
till he fell to his knees at Passchendaele,
grasping two fists-full of earth, a shell to the stomach
opening its scarlet blossom.

At the Eisteddfod they called his name three times,
his audience waiting to rise, thrilled,
to crown him, chair him,
to sing the hymn of peace,
not 'the festival in tears and the poet in his grave',
a black sheet placed across the empty chair.

HEDD WYN

War

Bitter to live in times like these.
While God declines beyond the seas;
Instead, man, king or peasantry,
Raises his gross authority.

When he thinks God has gone away
Man takes up his sword to slay
His brother; we can hear death's roar.
It shadows the hovels of the poor.

Like the old songs they left behind,
We hung our harps in the willows again.
Ballads of boys blow on the wind,
Their blood is mingled with the rain.

translated and chosen by GILLIAN CLARKE

Three Men

I

First, Joe, my mother's elder brother,
the clever lawyer. Clearing the house
after her death, I found two photos of him.
Their sepia tones made his face as soft as
a schoolboy's – but already too sensitive.

Dressed in a collegiate robe
and mortarboard, one of the photos
seems to celebrate a graduation.
In the other, his mouth is harder
and he looks a few years older,
but just as anxious. (He was
already married and a father).

Behind him hangs a painted backdrop
of army tents and a fluttering Stars
and Stripes. But someone had been careless
The flagpole seems to have impaled him,
rising from the top of Joe's head.

He's wearing uniform: greatcoat
and puttees, and holds a high-crowned hat

close against his thigh. Yet I find it
hard to imagine him as a doughboy.

What happened during basic training?
I was suspicious – although I never
learned exactly about the incident which
led to his discharge – but when he came home
he was different. Months later
he had his first spectacular breakdown,
which terrified his wife and children.
After a few more, he was sent
to one of those places for nervous diseases:
discreet, upstate, and not too expensive.
He never left.

II

The second man was Joe's son.
Another war had begun, and Stephen
was just old enough to be drafted.
He was sweet-natured and handsome.
I had a girlish crush on him.

It was lucky we were visiting
my aunt that day – how could we know
it was the last time we'd see him?
He had come to say goodbye to his
favourite aunt: the only family member
who encouraged him to be a poet.

Then once again, the training camp,
that place of danger for him and his father.
Once again, something happened.
This time, impossible to hide the facts.
He was run over by one of the same
group of recruits he trained with (maybe
even a friend). Half drunk, the youth
had climbed into the cab of an army truck
parked under the trees, which soon careened
out of control. Stephen, too close
to escape, was crushed to death.

III

Number three – the same scenario:
raw recruits and too much beer.
This is how my husband's uncle died,
not at the Battle of the Aisne, nor
in the senseless slaughter at Loos,
but on a moor in Norfolk. It can't
really be called collateral damage –
it was just boys being drunk and playful.

I never met him, but I know
(from stories my husband told)
that Oliver was one of those boys,
gentle and kind, loved by his sisters,
and mourned until the end of their lives.
I shared the grief, pity and rage
he still felt about his uncle's fate.

Because his father was a blacksmith,
Oliver was used to horses,
so was the one ordered to lead
a string of mules across the moor
at dusk. As a joke, some of his mates
fed rum to the mules – who went wild.
Trying to control them, a blow to the head
from a hoof downed him; they kicked him to death.
His body lay exposed on the moor
until it was found the next afternoon,
and sent back home for burial.

War destroyed these three men
who never reached a battlefield.

They never reached a battlefield,
But War destroyed these three men.

Three men who never reached a battlefield,
but War destroyed them.

The Second Coming

Turning and turning in the widening gyre
The falcon cannot hear the falconer;
Things fall apart; the centre cannot hold;
Mere anarchy is loosed upon the world,
The blood-dimmed tide is loosed, and everywhere
The ceremony of innocence is drowned;
The best lack all conviction, while the worst
Are full of passionate intensity.

Surely some revelation is at hand;
Surely the Second Coming is at hand:
The Second Coming! Hardly are those words out
When a vast image out of *Spiritus Mundi*
Troubles my sight: somewhere in sands of the desert
A shape with lion body and the head of a man,
A gaze blank and pitiless as the sun,
Is moving its slow thighs, while all about it
Reel shadows of the indignant desert birds.
The darkness drops again; but now I know
That twenty centuries of stony sleep
Were vexed to nightmare by a rocking cradle,
And what rough beast, its hour come round at last,
Slouches towards Bethlehem to be born?

chosen by RUTH FAINLIGHT

CAROL ANN DUFFY

Last Post

In all my dreams, before my helpless sight,
He plunges at me, guttering, choking, drowning.

If poetry could tell it backwards, true, begin
that moment shrapnel scythed you to the stinking mud . . .
but you get up, amazed, watch bled bad blood
run upwards from the slime into its wounds;
see lines and lines of British boys rewind
back to their trenches, kiss the photographs from home –
mothers, sweethearts, sisters, younger brothers
not entering the story now
to die and die and die.
Dulce – No – Decorum – No – Pro patria mori.
You walk away.

You walk away; drop your gun (fixed bayonet)
like all your mates do too –
Harry, Tommy, Wilfred, Edward, Bert –
and light a cigarette.
There's coffee in the square,
warm French bread
and all those thousands dead
are shaking dried mud from their hair
and queuing up for home. Freshly alive,

a lad plays Tipperary to the crowd, released
from History; the glistening, healthy horses fit for heroes, kings.

You lean against a wall,
your several million lives still possible
and crammed with love, work, children, talent, English beer,
    good food.
You see the poet tuck away his pocket-book and smile.

If poetry could truly tell it backwards,
then it would.

ACKNOWLEDGEMENTS

Faber & Faber would like to thank the following authors and translators whose work appears in this anthology: John Agard; Anna Akhmatova; Guillaume Apollinaire; Simon Armitage; Cynthia Asquith; Gottfried Benn; Oliver Bernard; Rachael Boast; Sean Borodale; Beverley Bie Brahic; Vera Brittain; Rupert Brooke; Polly Clark; Gillian Clarke; Billy Collins; Julia Copus; Patrick Creagh; Imtiaz Dharker; Theo Dorgan; Carol Ann Duffy; Helen Dunmore; Ruth Fainlight; Vicki Feaver; Elaine Feinstein; Roy Fisher; Robert Graves; Ann Gray; Ivor Gurney; Michael Hamburger; David Harsent; Seamus Heaney; Judith Hemschemeyer; Michael Hofmann; Adam Horovitz; T. E. Hulme; Alan Jenkins; Jackie Kay; Francis Ledwidge; Michael Longley; Ewart Alan Mackintosh; Albert Marshall; Tom McAlindon; John McCauley; Paula Meehan; Charlotte Mew; Blake Morrison; Andrew Motion; Paul Muldoon; Daljit Nagra; Sarojini Naidu; Grace Nichols; Bernard O'Donoghue; Alice Oswald; Wilfred Owen; Ruth Padel; Clare Pollard; Margaret Postgate Cole; Deryn Rees-Jones; Isaac Rosenberg; Saki; Siegfried Sassoon; Gertrude Stein; Edward Thomas; Helen Thomas; Georg Trakl; Giuseppe Ungaretti; Hedd Wyn; and W. B. Yeats.

The publishers gratefully acknowledge permission to reprint copyright material in this book, as follows:

ANNA AKHMATOVA: 'July 1914' from *The Complete Poems of Anna Akhmatova*, translated by Judith Hemschemeyer and edited by Roberta Reeder (Canongate, 1998/Zephyr Press, 2006), translation copyright © 1989, 1992, 1997 Judith Hemschemeyer, reprinted by permission of Canongate Books Ltd and The Permissions Company, Inc. on behalf of Zephyr Press, www.zephyrpress.org

CYNTHIA ASQUITH: extract from *Diaries 1915–1918* (Hutchinson, 1968), reprinted by permission of The Random House Group Ltd

permission of David Higham Associates

HELEN THOMAS: extract from *Under Storm's Wing* (Carcanet, 1988), reprinted by permission of Mrs R. Vellender, for the Estate of Helen Thomas

GEORG TRAKL: 'Grodek' from *Grodek: a poem*, translated by Michael Hamburger (Scargill Press, 1989), reprinted by permission of The Michael Hamburger Trust

GIUSEPPE UNGARETTI: 'Clear Sky' from *Selected Poems of Giuseppe Ungaretti*, edited and translated by Patrick Creagh (Penguin, 1971), from the original Italian 'Sereno' by Giuseppe Ungaretti, from *Vita di un uomo – Tutti le poesie*, copyright © Arnoldo Mondadori Editore S. p. A., Milan, reprinted by permission of Arnoldo Mondadori Editore

Although we have tried to trace and contact all copyright holders, we will be pleased to correct any inadvertent errors or omissions.

INDEX OF AUTHORS

INDEX OF TITLES AND FIRST LINES